HALLOWEEN!
TRICKS, TREATS, FUN & SWEETS

HALLOWEEN!
TRICKS, TREATS, FUN & SWEETS

25 seasonal ideas for all the family, with 100 photographs

LORENZ BOOKS

This edition is published by Lorenz Books,
an imprint of Anness Publishing Ltd,
Blaby Road, Wigston, Leicestershire LE18 4SE;
info@anness.com

www.lorenzbooks.com; www.annesspublishing.com

If you like the images in this book and would like
to investigate using them for publishing, promotions
or advertising, please visit our website
www.practicalpictures.com for more information.

Publisher: Joanna Lorenz
Project Editor: Emma Clegg
Introduction by Jeremy Smith
Editorial readers: Kate Henderson and Hayley Kerr
Designer: Mark Latter
Production Controller: Mai-Ling Collyer
Recipes by Norma Miller (p24), Roz Denny (p14), Linda
Fraser (p16), Elizabeth Wolf Cohen (p18), Stephanie
Donaldson (p19 and 20), Pamela Westland (p24), Bridget
Jones (p26 and 31), Angela Nilsen (p28), Joanna Farrow
(p32 and 35) and consultant editor Fiona Eaton (p36)
Costumes by Petra Boase and face-painting by
Bettina Graham
Projects by Deborah Schneebeli-Morrell (p56, 58 and
60) and Tessa Evelegh (p61 and 62)
Photographers: David Armstrong, James Duncan, John
Freeman, Michelle Garrett, Nelson Hargreaves, Amanda
Heywood, David Jordan, Michael Michaels and
Debbie Patterson

PUBLISHER'S NOTE
Although the advice and information in this book are
believed to be accurate and true at the time of going to
press, neither the authors nor the publisher can accept
any legal responsibility or liability for any errors or omis-
sions that may have been made nor for any inaccuracies
nor for any loss, harm or injury that comes about from
following instructions or advice in this book.

Contents

Introduction

The origins of Halloween can be traced back to the Celts, who inhabited many parts of the British Isles and Northern France. They traditionally celebrated a holiday called Samhain, marking the end of the harvest season and the beginning of the cold winter. It was believed that on the night of Samhain, witches, ghosts and other dark forces ruled, and that the souls of the dead would revisit the places where they had once dwelt. Huge fires were built to ward off the witches and spirits, but food and lanterns were set out to welcome the ghosts and souls of the dead.

In an effort to stamp out such pagan rituals, the Catholic Church decreed November 1st to be All Saints' Day, and the preceding evening All Hallows' Eve. However, the rather austere and sombre occasion of All Saints was no match for the riotous celebrations that had ushered in Halloween, and many still genuinely feared that malevolent forces at work on October 31st could overwhelm them if traditional customs were not followed.

In later years, Halloween became associated with further rituals, many invented by the Irish, such as trick or treating, where money or food was left on the houseowner's doorstep for those wearing Halloween disguises. The ritual was then adopted in America with the arrival of nineteenth-century Irish immigrants, and today "trick or treating" is popular the world over.

The tradition of Halloween is still celebrated throughout the world with party games and disguises, seasonal recipes, and decorative displays. The menace and devilment that once invested Halloween have now given way to a spirit of light-heartedness which sees children making mischief and cajoling gifts and treats out of resigned adults.

This book will help you and your family to celebrate the lighter side of Halloween, and contains a range of ideas to make the festival or party a truly memorable occasion. The projects featured use familiar motifs to enchant you, such as pumpkins, ghosts, black cats and witches. There are seasonal pies, tarts and sweets to warm you through, and ghoulish disguises to delight and terrify all those who come into contact with them. *Halloween* will ensure that this traditional time of year retains its former reputation for fiendish fun.

Simple Party Ideas

Almost as soon as the days turn damp, chill and gloomy, and the nights start to draw in,
it is time to plan your Halloween party. This is a great opportunity to involve the children,
so take a step back from reality and let your imaginations run wild.

Devilish Table

Decorate your table with the frightful images of Halloween. Children will love to help you set this table!

* Cover the table completely with black crepe paper, running the sheets widthways over the table. Use double-sided tape to attach wide black satin ribbon over the joins in the paper and tie black bows to finish the ends of the ribbon.

* Use pumpkin lanterns to light up the table, placing them on small thick cork mats or pot stands.

* Cut out witches in black cardboard, adding an extra 5cm/2in to the bottom and folding this back so that the witches stand up. Weight the flap with a small piece of blue tack (a pliable adhesive such as Funtac) or Plasticine. Stand the witches towards the back of the buffet table set back against a wall.

Spooky Lights

Scoop out the insides of several small pumpkins. Then cut out holes for eyes, a nose and gap teeth. Place a small candle in the middle of the shell and replace the lid. Place them around the house to create a Halloween atmosphere.

Dancing Witches

Make enough of these spooky witches to stretch across the room.

* For the template, draw a witch on a rectangle of card (posterboard), so that parts of the shape touch the rectangle sides. Cut out the witch.

* Cut a strip of black crepe paper as wide as the long sides of the rectangle. Fold it accordion-style, in pleats the same width as the template. Place the template on the folded paper, draw around it and cut it out, taking care to leave the shapes joined at the sides. Unfold the pleats to reveal the dancing witches.

House of Horrors

Completely darken one room, play creepy music and guide two or three children at a time to the delights of:

* Peeled grapes – "eyes".
* Cooked, cold spaghetti – "brains".
* Yogurt – "ghost slime".
* Dried pear slices – "ears".
* Home-made cobwebs and large spiders hung everywhere.
* A "ghost" which pops from behind a chair or out of a cupboard. (Get an older sibling to dress up.)

Warming Delights

This chapter is partly a celebration of the humble pumpkin – that versatile vegetable with its rich colour, slightly sweet flesh and a shell which, when hollowed out, makes an attractive serving bowl. Most importantly, however, you will discover a delicious sampling of warming recipes to tempt your guests, to give a nutritious glow to your Halloween celebration and keep out the winter chills. These recipes introduce a soup recipe and savoury dishes, sweet pumpkin pie, muffins and fritters, all presented in party portions. Here is everything you need for a Halloween feast.

Pumpkin Soup

Start a seasonal meal with this soup, which has all the elements of a great winter soup – a glorious colour, a rich and creamy texture and, not least, a delicious, spicy flavour.

Ingredients

1.5kg/3–3½lb pumpkin
60ml/4 tbsp olive oil
4 large onions, sliced
2 garlic cloves, crushed
4 fresh red chillies,
seeded and chopped
10ml/2 tsp curry paste
1.5 litres/2½ pints/6¼ cups
vegetable or chicken stock
300ml/½ pint/1¼ cups single
(light) cream
salt and ground black pepper

Serves 8

TIP
Use hollowed-out
small squashes or
pumpkins as
individual soup bowls.

1. Peel the pumpkin, remove the seeds and chop the flesh roughly.

2. Heat the oil in a large saucepan and fry the onions until golden. Stir in the garlic, chillies and curry paste. Cook for 1 minute, then add the chopped pumpkin and cook for a further 5 minutes.

3. Pour over the stock and season with salt and pepper. Bring to a boil, then cover and simmer for about 25 minutes.

4. Process until smooth in a food processor or blender, then return to the clean pan and reheat. Taste the mixture and add seasoning if necessary.

5. Serve the soup in heated individual bowls, adding a generous spoonful of cream to each portion. Hot bread makes an ideal accompaniment.

Autumn Glory

Golden pumpkin shells summon up the delights of autumn – use one as a serving pot for this delicious pumpkin and pasta partnership. Prepare the pumpkin and cook up to the end of step 4 up to a day ahead.

Ingredients

2 x 2kg/4lb pumpkins

2 onions, sliced

5cm/2in piece fresh ginger root, grated

90ml/6 tbsp extra virgin olive oil

2 courgettes (zucchini), sliced

225g/8oz sliced mushrooms

2 x 400g/14oz cans chopped tomatoes

150g/5oz/2 cups pasta shells

900ml/1½ pints/ 3¾ cups stock

120ml/8 tbsp fromage frais or ricotta cheese

60ml/4 tbsp chopped fresh basil

salt and ground black pepper

Serves 8

1. Preheat the oven to 180°C/350°F/Gas 4. Cut the tops off the pumpkins with a large sharp knife and then scoop out and discard the seeds.

2. Using a small sharp knife and a sturdy tablespoon or ice cream scoop, take out as much of the pumpkin flesh as possible. Then chop the pumpkin flesh into chunks.

3. Bake the pumpkins with the lids on for ¾–1 hour until the insides begin to soften.

4. Meanwhile, make the filling. Gently fry the onions, ginger and pumpkin in the olive oil for about 10 minutes, stirring occasionally.

5. Add the courgettes and mushrooms and cook for a further 3 minutes, then stir in the tomatoes, pasta shells and stock. Season well. Bring to a boil, then cover and simmer gently for 10 minutes until the pasta is just tender.

6. Stir the fromage frais or ricotta cheese and basil into the pasta mixture, then spoon the mixture into the pumpkin shells.

7. If it is not possible to fit the entire filling into the pumpkin shells, then serve the rest separately. Use the two pumpkins as the centrepiece of your table display.

Pumpkin Muffins

Pumpkin has a mild, sweet flavour and makes a delicious, moist muffin. As with most muffins, these are best eaten fresh, on the day they are made.

Ingredients

115g/4oz/8 tbsp butter or margarine, at room temperature

150ml/¼ pint/⅔ cup dark brown sugar, firmly packed

150ml/¼ pint/⅔ cup black treacle (molasses)

1 egg, at room temperature, beaten

225g/8oz/1 cup cooked or canned pumpkin

200g/7oz/1¾ cups plain (all-purpose) flour

1.25ml/¼ tsp salt

5ml/1 tsp bicarbonate of soda (baking soda)

7.5ml/1½ tsp ground cinnamon

5ml/1 tsp grated nutmeg

25g/1oz/¼ cup currants or raisins

Makes 14

1. Preheat the oven to 200°C/400°F/Gas 6. Grease 14 muffin cups or use paper liners. With an electric mixer, cream the butter or margarine until soft. Add the brown sugar and molasses and beat again until light and fluffy.

2. Add the egg and pumpkin and stir until they are well blended. Sift over the flour, salt, bicarbonate of soda and cinnamon and add the nutmeg. Fold them just enough to blend the ingredients without overmixing.

3. Fold in the currants or raisins. Spoon the batter into the prepared muffin cups, filling them three-quarters full.

4. Bake for about 12–15 minutes, until well risen and firm in the middle. Transfer to a wire rack. Serve warm or cold.

Corn and Ham Muffins

These delicious little muffins are really simple to make. If you like, serve them unfilled with a pot of herb butter.

Ingredients

60g/2¼oz/scant ½ cup yellow cornmeal

70g/2¼oz/⅔ cup plain (all-purpose) flour

30ml/2 tbsp sugar

7.5ml/1½ tsp baking powder

2.5ml/½ tsp salt

60g/2¼oz/4 tbsp butter, melted

120ml/4fl oz/½ cup whipping cream

1 egg, beaten

1–2 jalapeño or other medium-hot chillies, seeded and finely chopped (optional)

pinch cayenne pepper

butter for spreading

whole-grain mustard (or mustard with honey) for spreading

60g/2¼oz oak-(hickory) smoked ham

Makes 24

1. Preheat the oven to 200°C/400°F/Gas 6 and grease a muffin tin with 24 4cm/1½in cups. Combine the cornmeal, flour, sugar, baking powder and salt. In another bowl, whisk together the melted butter, cream, beaten egg, chillies and cayenne pepper.

2. Make a well, pour in the egg mixture and stir into the dry ingredients just enough to blend (do not overmix).

3. Drop 15ml/1 tbsp batter into the muffin cups. Bake for 12–15 minutes, until golden and just firm. Cool the tin slightly on a wire rack, then turn out the muffins to cool.

4. Split the muffins and spread each bottom half with a little butter and mustard. Cut out small rounds of ham with a pastry (cookie) cutter and place them on the muffins. Replace the tops of the muffins.

Pumpkin Fritters

These moist and delicious fritters should be eaten while still hot, liberally
sprinkled with cinnamon sugar.

1. Soak the sultanas in warm water or
brandy for about 15 minutes, then drain
them well.

2. Place the pumpkin, flour, sugar, baking
powder, salt and lemon rind in a food
processor and blend thoroughly until the
mixture is smooth.

3. Stir in the sultanas, mixing lightly to
incorporate air into the batter.

4. Heat the oil in a frying pan and drop
walnut-size spoonfuls of mixture into the
hot oil. Cook briefly, turning once, until the
fritters are lightly browned. Serve warm,
sprinkled with cinnamon sugar.

Ingredients

75g/3oz sultanas
(golden raisins)
brandy (optional)
450g/1lb pumpkin, cooked
and drained
50g/2oz/$\frac{1}{2}$ cup plain
(all-purpose) flour,
sifted twice
15ml/1 tbsp soft
light brown sugar
2.5ml/$\frac{1}{2}$ tsp baking powder
pinch of salt
finely grated rind of 1 lemon
oil for frying
cinnamon sugar, for
sprinkling
Makes 16–20

TIP

Make fritters up to
one day in advance
and then reheat in a
hot oven for 15–20
minutes.

Pumpkin Pie

Why wait for Thanksgiving – this luxurious version of pumpkin pie is a
traditional end to a Halloween meal and perfect for those with a sweet tooth.

Ingredients

450g/1lb pumpkin

375g/13oz ready-made
shortcrust pastry

175g/6oz brown sugar

175ml/6fl oz/¾ cup milk

4 eggs

250ml/8fl oz/1 cup double
(heavy) cream

50ml/2fl oz/¼ cup brandy

10ml/2 tsp ground cinnamon

2.5ml/½ tsp ground ginger
or grated nutmeg

2.5ml/½ tsp salt

Serves 8

TIP

Prepare pastry case
up to one day ahead
(or freeze for up to
one month). Prepare
filling up to two days
in advance.

1. Using a large sharp knife, chop the
pumpkin flesh into small pieces.

2. Steam the cubed pumpkin for about
10-15 minutes until soft. Leave to drain,
preferably overnight.

3. Line a 25cm/10in flan tin (tart pan) with
pastry and chill for 15 minutes.

4. Preheat the oven to 180°C/350°F/Gas 4.

5. Place the drained pumpkin in a food
processor with all the remaining ingredients
and blend to a smooth purée.

6. Pour the filling into the prepared pastry
case and bake for 1¼ hours until set.

Bewitching Sweets

Trick or treat – there are no tricks or special techniques here, just some simple recipes for delicious, sweet treats. Make a batch of Cranberry Fudge, or some special orange Marshmallows to offer to the ghouls and witches that come to your door. Alternatively bake the intriguing Gingerbread Cookies and one of our theme cakes for a Halloween tea party. And don't forget the Toffee Apples for your guests to take home!

Cranberry Fudge

Everybody loves fudge. You can make a variety of flavours by replacing the cranberries with chopped pecans, walnuts or hazelnuts, candied ginger or other candied fruits.

Ingredients

900g/2 lb/4 cups granulated (white) sugar

50g/2oz/¼ cup unsalted butter

175ml/6fl oz/¾ cup milk

15ml/1 tbsp golden (light corn) syrup

200g/7oz can condensed milk

115g/4oz/¾ cup fresh cranberries

Makes 900g/2lb

1. Place the sugar, butter, milk and golden syrup in a heavy saucepan and bring slowly to a boil, stirring constantly. Add the condensed milk, return to a boil, still stirring, until the mixture reaches 130°C/250°F on a sugar (candy) thermometer, or the "hardball stage" (see Tip, below).

2. Remove the pan from the heat and stir in the fresh cranberries. Pour the mixture into a well-greased Swiss roll tin (jelly roll pan). Mark the fudge into squares just before it hardens. When the fudge is cold, break it into pieces and store them in an airtight container.

TIP

To test the mixture without a sugar (candy) thermometer, drop a small spoonful into a cup of cold water. At the correct temperature, the "hardball stage", the mixture will set hard.

Spellbound Tart

This unusual Halloween tart is a chocolate-lover's
fantasy – children and adults alike will be entranced.

Ingredients

175g/6oz/1½ cups plain
(all-purpose) flour
115g/4oz/½ cup
unsalted butter, diced
50g/2oz/¼ cup caster
(superfine) sugar, for the base
50g/2oz/½ cup hazelnuts,
chopped and toasted
45ml/3 tbsp cocoa powder
2 eggs, separated
30ml/2 tbsp water
300ml/½ pint/1¼ cups milk
25g/1oz/3 tbsp cornflour
(cornstarch)
15ml/1 tbsp caster (superfine)
sugar, for the filling
225g/8oz white chocolate drops
or chips
5ml/1 tsp natural vanilla extract
150ml/¼ pint/⅔ cup double
(heavy) cream
225g/8oz/8 squares
milk chocolate

Serves 8

1. Sift the flour and rub (cut) in the butter.
Stir in the sugar, hazelnuts and cocoa, then
add one egg yolk and the water. Use a knife
to mix the egg and water into the mixture
to bind it into a soft dough.

2. Roll out the pastry and use to line a
25cm/10in loose-bottomed flan tin (tart
pan). Trim away the excess pastry and prick
the base, then chill for 30 minutes. Preheat
the oven to 200°C/400°F/Gas 6.

3. Line the pastry case (shell) with non-
stick baking paper and beans, and bake for
20 minutes. Remove the paper and beans
and bake for a further 10 minutes.

4. Mix a little milk with the cornflour and
caster sugar until smooth. Bring the
remaining milk to a boil, then pour it
on to the cornflour mixture, stirring all
the time. Return the sauce to the pan
and bring it back to a boil, stirring
continuously. Simmer for 3 minutes,
stirring, until the sauce is very thick.
Remove from the heat.

5. Add the second egg yolk and the
chocolate drops or chips and stir until the
chocolate melts. Stir in the vanilla extract
then cover the surface of the sauce with
wetted non-stick baking paper. Leave it to
just cool, rather than set.

6. Beat the sauce to remove lumps. Whip
the cream until it stands in soft peaks, then
fold it into the sauce. Beat the egg whites
until they stand in stiff peaks and fold them
into the mixture. Turn the mixture into the
pastry case, swirl it around evenly and chill
the tart for a few hours.

7. Trace witch shapes on to non-stick baking paper using a felt-tip pen. Turn the paper over, securing the corners on a board with tape. Melt the chocolate in a bowl over a small saucepan of hot, not boiling, water. Make a paper piping bag and spoon some chocolate into it.

8. Fold the end down to seal and cut the tip off the bag. Carefully outline the witch shapes. Enlarge the hole and flood the shapes completely, using a cocktail stick (toothpick) to ease the chocolate into the corners. When set, use a palette knife to lift the chocolate witch shapes on to the tart.

Pumpkin Cake

Halloween is a time for spooky cakes – and this one is very popular with children. Make this and you are all set for a party full of eerie surprises.

1. To make a Madeira cake mixture, preheat the oven to 160°C/325°F/Gas 3. Grease and line the bases of two 1.2 litres/2½ pints/5 cups pudding bowls.

2. Sift the flour and baking powder into a mixing bowl. Add the sugar, margarine, eggs and milk. Mix together with a wooden spoon, then beat for 1–2 minutes until smooth and glossy.

3. Divide the mixture equally between the pudding bowls and spread evenly. Give the bowls a sharp tap to remove any air pockets. Make a depression in the centre of the mixture to ensure a level surface once the cakes are cooked. Bake for 1¼ hours. Turn out and cool on a wire rack.

4. Trim the widest ends of each cake so they will fit flat against one another to make a round shape. Split each cake in half horizontally and fill with some of the butter icing, then stick the two cakes together with butter icing to form a pumpkin shape.

5. Trim one of the narrow ends slightly, to give a better pumpkin shape. Make this the bottom of the pumpkin. Cover the outside of the cake with the remaining butter icing.

▶

Ingredients

225g/8oz/2 cups plain (all-purpose) flour
5ml/1 tsp baking powder
175g/6oz/¾ cup caster (superfine) sugar
175g/6oz/¾ cup soft margarine
3 eggs
30ml/2 tbsp milk
250g/9oz orange-flavoured butter icing (frosting)
450 g/1lb sugarpaste icing (fondant)
125g/4oz royal icing (frosting)
orange, black and yellow food colouring
cornflour (cornstarch) for dusting

Serves 15

6. Take 350g/12oz of the sugarpaste and colour it orange. Roll out thinly on a surface lightly dusted with cornflour and use to cover the cake, trimming to fit. Mould it gently to give a smooth surface.

7. Mark the pumpkin segments using a thin wooden skewer. With a fine paintbrush and watered-down orange food colouring, paint on the markings for the flesh. Use orange sugar paste icing trimmings for the top of the cake where the witch bursts out: cut and tear rolled out pieces to create jagged edges. Attach to the cake with a little water.

TIP
Kept in an airtight container, this cake will stay fresh for up to 3 days. Freezing is not recommended.

8. Colour three-quarters of the remaining sugarpaste black. Of the remainder, colour a little yellow and leave the rest white. Use some of the black and white sugarpaste to make the witch, moulding the head, arms and body separately and securing with royal icing. When set, roll out some black sugarpaste and cut jagged edges to form a cape. Drape over the arms and body, securing with a little water.

9. Make the hat in two pieces – a circle and a cone – and secure with royal icing. Leave to dry on non-stick baking parchment. Shape the cauldron, broomstick and cat's head out of more black and yellow sugar paste, securing the handle of the cauldron with royal icing. Leave to dry on non-stick baking paper.

10. Roll out the remaining black sugar paste for the features. Cut out eyes, nose and mouth and attach to the pumpkin with a little water. Place the cake on a 23cm/9in round cake board, secure the witch on top with royal icing and arrange the cat, cauldron and broomstick around the base.

Toffee Apples

Toffee (caramel) apples are a traditional offering at Halloween. Give one of these prettily wrapped toffee apples to each child as they leave after the party.

1. Combine the sugar and water in a heavy saucepan. Heat gently, stirring, until the sugar has dissolved. Do not allow the syrup to boil. Wash any sugar crystals off the sides of the pan with a brush dipped in cold water, then bring the syrup to a boil. Do not stir the syrup while it is boiling, or the sugar may crystallize.

2. Boil the syrup until it turns golden, then quickly remove it from the heat and dip the base of the pan in cold water to stop the syrup getting darker.

3. Dip the apples in the caramel, turning them on their sticks to coat them evenly. Allow excess syrup to drip off, then twirl the apples and place on oiled foil.

Ingredients

900g/2lb/4 cups sugar

300ml/½ pint/
1¼ cups water

8–12 apples, each skewered
with a sturdy wooden stick

Makes 8–12

TIP

Once the caramel has set, wrap each apple in clear cellophane and tie with a ribbon bow. Pile the toffee apples in a basket and watch them disappear.

Ghost Cake

This children's cake is really simple to make yet very effective. Use a square
cake of your choice, such as a citrus- or chocolate-flavoured Madeira,
or a light fruit cake.

1. Preheat the oven to 150°C/300°F/
Gas 2. Grease and line the base of an
18cm/7in square cake tin (pan) with
greased greaseproof (wax) paper.
Grease and line the base of a 300ml/
½ pint/1¼ cups pudding basin (deep bowl)
with greaseproof paper.

2. To make an orange-flavoured quick-mix
sponge cake, sift the flour and baking
powder into a bowl. Add sugar, margarine
and eggs. Mix together with a wooden
spoon, then beat the mixture for 1–2
minutes until smooth and glossy. Stir in the
orange flavouring and beat thoroughly
until evenly blended.

3. Half-fill the basin with cake mixture
and turn the remaining mix into
the cake tin. Bake the basin for
25 minutes and the tin for 1½ hours.
Allow to cool.

4. Knead a little black food colouring into
125g/4oz of the sugarpaste icing and use
to cover a 23cm/9in round cake board.
Trim off the excess.

5. Cut two small corners off the large
cake. Cut two larger wedges off the other
two corners. Stand the large cake on the
iced board. Halve the larger cake
trimmings and wedge them around the
base of the cake. ▶

Ingredients

225g/8oz/2 cups self-raising
(self-rising) flour
10ml/2 tsp baking powder
225g/8oz/1 cup caster
(superfine) sugar
225g/8oz/1 cup soft
margarine
4 eggs
orange flavouring
900g/2lb sugarpaste icing
(fondant)
350g/12oz butter icing
(frosting)
black food colouring
cornflour (cornstarch) for
dusting

Serves 14

TIP

This sponge cake can
be frozen for up to two
months. Covered
loosely in foil and
stored in a cool, dry
place, the iced (frosted)
cake will keep for up to
two weeks.

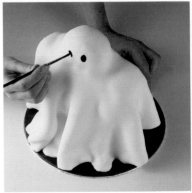

6. Secure the smaller cake to the top of the larger one with butter icing. Use the remaining icing to cover the cake.

7. Roll out the remaining sugarpaste icing on a surface dusted with cornflour to an oval shape about 51cm/20in long and 30cm/12in wide.

8. Lay the icing on the cake, letting it fall in folds. Smooth the sugarpaste icing over the top half and trim any excess.

9. Using black food colouring, paint two oval eyes on to the head.

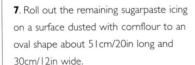

Gingerbread Cookies

These pretty cookies are deceptively easy to make, and are the perfect, spicy addition to a Halloween party. They would also make a lovely gift.

1. Sift together the flour, bicarbonate of soda, salt and spices for the golden gingerbread. Rub the butter into the mixture. Add the sugar, syrup and egg yolk and mix to a firm dough. Knead, wrap and chill. Use the same method for the chocolate gingerbread mixture.

2. Roll out half the chocolate dough on a floured surface to a 28 x 4cm/11 x 1½in rectangle, 1cm/½in thick. Repeat with the golden gingerbread dough. Cut both lengths into seven long, thin strips. Lay the strips side by side, alternating the colours.

3. Roll out the remaining golden gingerbread dough to a long sausage, 2cm/¾in wide and the length of the strips. Lay the sausage of dough down the centre of the striped dough. Carefully bring the striped dough up around the sausage and press gently to enclose the sausage. Roll the remaining chocolate dough to a thin rectangle measuring 28 x 13cm/11 x 5in.

4. Bring the chocolate dough around the striped dough and press into place. Wrap in greaseproof (wax) paper and chill.

5. Preheat the oven to 180°C/350 °F/ Gas 4. Grease a large baking sheet. Cut the gingerbread roll into thin slices and place on the baking sheet. Bake for about 12-15 minutes, until just beginning to colour.

Ingredients

Golden gingerbread:
175g/6oz/1½ cups plain flour
1.5ml/1/4 tsp bicarbonate of soda (baking soda)
pinch of salt
5ml/1 tsp ground ginger
5ml/1 tsp ground cinnamon
65g/2½oz unsalted butter
75g/3oz caster (superfine) sugar
30ml/2 tbsp golden syrup
1 egg yolk, beaten
Chocolate gingerbread:
175g/6oz/1½ cups plain flour
pinch of salt
10ml/2 tsp mixed spice
2.5ml/½ tsp bicarbonate of soda (baking soda)
25g/1oz cocoa powder
75g/3oz/6 tbsp unsalted butter
75g/3oz light muscovado sugar
1 egg
Makes about 25

Marshmallows

Home–made marshmallows are a special treat. Make them at Halloween with orange flower water and flavouring and then toast them before serving.

Ingredients

45g/1¾oz icing (confectioners') sugar

45g/1¾oz/7 tbsp cornflour (cornstarch)

50ml/2fl oz/¼ cup cold water

45ml/3 tbsp orange flower water

25g/1oz powdered gelatine

450g/1lb/2 cups granulated (white) sugar

30ml/2 tbsp liquid glucose

250ml/8fl oz/1 cup boiling water

2 egg whites

orange food colouring

Makes 500g/1¼lb

TIP

For pink marshmallows, substitute rose water and pink food colouring for the orange flower water and orange food colouring.

1. Lightly oil a 28 × 18cm/11 × 7in Swiss roll tin (jelly roll pan). Sift together the icing sugar and cornflour and use some of this mixture to evenly coat the inside of the tin (pan). Shake out the excess.

2. Mix together the cold water, orange flower water, gelatine and a drop of orange food colouring in a small bowl. Place over a saucepan of hot water and stir occasionally until the gelatine has dissolved.

3. Place the sugar, liquid glucose and boiling water in a heavy saucepan. Stir over a low heat to dissolve the sugar completely. Make sure that there are no sugar crystals around the water line; if so, wash these down with a brush dipped in cold water.

4. Bring the sugar syrup to a boil and boil steadily without stirring until the temperature reaches 127°C/260°F on a sugar (candy) thermometer. Remove from the heat and stir in the gelatine mixture.

5. While the syrup is boiling, whisk the egg whites until stiff. Pour a stream of syrup on to the egg whites while whisking for about 3 minutes or until the mixture is thick and foamy. Add more food colouring if the mixture looks pale.

6. Pour the mixture into the tin and allow to set. Sift the remaining icing sugar over the marshmallow surface and over a board. Ease the mixture away using an oiled palette knife (metal spatula) and invert on to the board. Cut into 2.5cm/1in squares, coating the cut sides with the icing sugar.

Spooky Disguises

Halloween just wouldn't be the same without the dressing up, and yet the usual last-minute scramble for a costume often has disappointing results. However, with a bit of forethought and some basic materials and make-up, you can transform children with these stunning outfits. You really need no more than an hour or so to create any one of these costumes; the only difficult part is choosing which one!

Ghost

The classic, spooky, floaty costume. Some fluorescent paint, judiciously applied, would make the ghost glow in the dark.

You will need

old white sheet

scissors

needle and thread or sewing machine

milliner's wire

black felt

fabric glue

1. Cut two pieces of sheet in the shape of a semi-circle, making sure the height is greater than your own height. Sew the two pieces together, leaving an opening at the bottom. Sew another line of stitching parallel to the line you have sewn. This is to make a tube for the wire.

2. Thread the wire through the tube. Cut the wire at each end of the tube and secure both ends of the wire to the sheet with a few stitches. This will stop the wire from coming free and scratching you.

3. Cut out a mouth and a pair of eyes from a piece of felt and glue them on to the sheet using fabric glue.

4. Cut small holes in the eyes and mouth, so that you can see where you are going and also so that you can breathe comfortably. Try the costume on and bend the wire to fit your body.

Frankenstein's Monster

This costume should be worn in combination with a well-practised "monster walk" to really send the shivers up onlookers' spines.

1. Using a damp sponge, apply the base colour over the face. Rinse the sponge, then apply a darker shade, avoiding the mouth and nose area. Finally, shade the cheekbones with a third colour.

4. Using a fine brush, paint a black scar on the forehead and on one side of the face. Put on a black swimming hat, making sure you hide most of the hair. Finally paint a jagged hair line where the hat meets the forehead.

You will need

make-up sponge

water-based face paints

medium make-up brush

fine make-up brush

black swimming hat (bathing cap)

2. Using a medium brush, paint the eyebrows black and darken the eyelids and the area under each eye.

3. Paint the lips black and, using a fine brush, paint fine black lines at either side of the mouth.

Witch

This wild young witch is keeping some secret spells under her hat! Complete the look with a cloak made from fabric, and long, black artificial nails.

You will need

tape measure

black fabric for hat

iron-on interfacing (optional)

pencil

scissors

needle and thread or sewing machine

raffia or straw

lipstick brush

water-based face paints

thick make-up brush

1. To make the hat, measure the width of your head so that you know how wide to make the rim of the hat. If the fabric you are using needs to be stiffened, iron a piece of interfacing on to the reverse side. Ask an adult to help you. Draw and cut out a triangle with a curved base, making sure the rim measures the width of your head, plus a small allowance for sewing the fabric together.

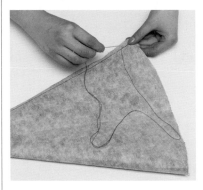

2. With the right sides facing, fold the triangle in half to form a tall cone and sew along the side.

3. Make bundles of raffia or straw and tie a knot in the centre of each one. Sew the knots around the hat's rim, leaving a gap at the front. Turn the hat the right way out.

4. With a lipstick brush, paint a pair of wild, black eyebrows. Paint a black line on each eyelid just above the eyelashes, a line of red under each eye and a black curve below.

5. Add ageing lines. Build more colour on to the cheeks using a thick make-up brush. Paint the lips red, exaggerating the top lip.

Skeleton

This is the perfect outfit for spooking your friends and family. Wear it if you dare! Try painting the skeleton on front and back for all-round spookiness.

You will need

black leotard

black leggings

white fabric paints

paintbrush

black make-up (eye-liner)

pencil

water-based face paints

medium make-up brush

1. Using fabric paints, draw the outline of the skeleton's ribcage, backbone and pelvis on the leotard. Make sure that the leotard stays flat as you work.

2. Paint the outline of the skeleton's leg bones on the front of the leggings.

3. Using a paintbrush and white fabric paint, fill in the outlines of the bones on both the leotard and leggings. Allow the paint to dry completely before trying the outfit on.

4. Using a black make-up pencil, draw a circular outline around each eye, a small triangle above each nostril, and a large mouth shape around the mouth.

5. Using a medium brush, paint the face white, avoiding the black shapes.

6. Paint black the eyes, the triangles above the nostrils, the sides of the face and around the mouth. Paint the mouth area white. Use black lines to divide the mouth into a set of ghoulish teeth.

Vampire

When this disguise is worn with an all-black outfit, friends and family are certain to be terrified by such haunting looks.

1. Using a damp sponge, apply a base colour to the face. Rinse the sponge, then dab a slightly darker shade on the forehead, blending it with the base colour.

2. Using a medium brush, paint a black triangle in the centre of the forehead, another triangle on either side of the face at the cheekbones and a small one at the bottom of the chin. You might find it easier to draw the outline for each shape first, to make sure they are symmetrical, and then fill them in afterwards.

3. Using a fine brush, paint a pair of jagged eyebrows over the model's own. Paint the eyelids white and the area up to the eyebrows grey.

4. Colour the area under the eyes red. Exaggerate the points on the top lip and colour the lips black.

5. Outline two fangs under the bottom lip and colour them yellow. Dab fake blood or red make-up at the points of the fangs and at the corners of the eyes.

You will need

make-up sponge

water-based face paints

medium make-up brush

fine make-up brush

black make-up (eye-liner) pencil (optional)

red make-up (lip-liner) pencil (optional)

fake blood (optional)

Cat

Paint on some feline features, dress up in a black leotard – perhaps even add a pair of black furry ears – and a tail and you will then be the slinkiest and most glamorous cat in town!

You will need

make-up sponge

water-based face paints

medium make-up brush

fine make-up brush

thick make-up brush

blusher

1. Using a damp sponge, apply a white base over the whole face. Using a medium brush, paint a border of black spikes around the edge of the face. You might find it easier to draw the outline first and then fill it in afterwards.

2. Paint a black outline around the eyes as shown in the next picture and paint the eyebrows thick and black.

3. Gently paint the eyelids and inside the black outline in a bright colour. Do not apply make-up too close to the eyelashes. Paint above the eyes.

4. Paint a black heart on the nose tip, a thin line from nose to chin (avoiding the mouth) and whisker spots under the nose.

5. Paint the lips a bright colour. Using a thick brush, dust each cheek with blusher.

Egyptian Mummy

Make sure that a white T–shirt and a pair of leggings or white tights are worn underneath the costume, just in case it starts to unravel.

You will need

old white sheet
scissors
needle and thread
white T-shirt
leggings or tights
make-up sponge
water-based face paints

1. To make the costume, tear or cut the sheet into strips about 10cm/4in wide and as long as possible.

2. Sew the strips of fabric together to form one long strip.

3. For the face, use a damp sponge to apply a white base. Rinse the sponge, then dab light purple around the eye sockets.

4. Wrap the fabric around the circle of the face. Then wrap the fabric round the head first. Leaving the face open, gradually wrap the fabric down the body.

5. When you reach the hands, go back up the arm again, wrapping the fabric as you go. Do the same with the feet and legs. When you have wrapped the whole body, sew the end of the strip to the costume. To take the costume off, simply cut the end free and unravel the fabric strip.

Robot

The fun part of this project is collecting all the bits and pieces to recycle. Ask your friends and family to help you collect interesting boxes and packages.

You will need

2 cardboard (paperboard) boxes
pencil
scissors
silver spray paint
assorted cartons and containers made of cardboard (paperboard)
clear plastic glue
Christmas ornaments
foil pie-dishes (pans)
masking tape
pair of old shoes
2 metal kitchen scourers (scrubbers)
tin foil

1. To make the helmet you will need a cardboard box that fits comfortably over your head. Draw a square on one side and cut it out.

2. Make sure the box is sprayed silver with an adult. This should be done outdoors or in a very airy room where the surfaces are covered. When the paint has dried, glue a clear plastic carton over the square hole. Punch a few holes in the plastic to let the air through.

3. Decorate the box by gluing on a range of assorted Christmas ornaments and foil pie-dishes.

4. For the robot's body you will need a large cardboard box. Cut a hole in the top of the box for your head and one on either side for your arms. Secure the edges of the holes with masking tape.

5. Decorate the robot body by gluing on boxes and containers. When the glue has dried, spray the box silver, following the same instructions as in step 2. Leave the paint to dry completely before you try on the costume.

6. Spray the shoes silver and decorate them with the metal kitchen scourers or anything shiny. Finally, when you are dressed in your costume, ask a friend to wrap your arms and legs in tin foil.

Festive Displays

The projects in this chapter offer creative ways to use seasonal fruits and vegetables, colours and images to develop the festive theme of Halloween in your home. Along with several cleverly carved pumpkins, the autumnal Candle Holders shed a wider light, and the Autumn Apple Display is beautiful both fresh and dried and will never lose its charm — it can be used again and again and will work its magic on even the most modest of dining rooms.

Jack O'Lantern

Let everyone carve a different Halloween face to create a whole crowd of characters. Give them hats if you like, such as Jack's small pumpkin bobble hat.

You will need

water-soluble crayon
Red Kuri squash
kitchen knife
ice-cream scoop
fine black pen
craft knife
gimlet
lino (linoleum)-cutting tool
small pumpkin or squash

I. Using the crayon, draw a circle about 9cm/3½in in diameter on the top of the Red Kuri squash. Cut out using the kitchen knife. Scoop out the seeds and flesh with the ice-cream scoop, leaving a shell 1cm/½in thick. Draw the features on to one side of the squash with the pen.

2. Using the craft knife, cut the nose and eyebrows in one line. Cut away the whites of the eyes. Use the gimlet to make a hole in the centre of each eye.

3. Use the lino-cutting tool to cut out the moustache. Cut the space between the teeth with the craft knife.

4. Cut a circle in the base of the small pumpkin and hollow out. Draw scrolls on the pumpkin.

5. Use the craft knife to cut the scrolls into curling slits. Stand a lighted candle or night-light (tea-light) inside the large shell, then place the small pumpkin on the top.

Little Pumpkins

Keep carving designs simple on the smaller pumpkins, lending variety with slits, zigzags and scrolls. Make several of them, then group together in an evocative Halloween window display.

You will need

fine black pen

small pumpkins or squashes

craft knife

teaspoon

1. Using the pen, draw a circle on the base of each pumpkin. Cut out using the craft knife. Scoop out the flesh with the teaspoon.

2. Draw zigzags on one pumpkin and cut away with the craft knife. The slits should be 5mm/¼in wide in the middle, tapering to points at both ends.

3. Draw and cut straight slits on another pumpkin.

4. For the scroll design, first draw on the shape, then carefully cut it away using the craft knife.

Feline Friends

Pale-skinned pumpkins make great canvases for all sorts of characters. This design provides a witty twist to the traditional Halloween witch's cat.

You will need

tracing paper and pen

White Boer or other pale-skinned pumpkin

dressmaker's (straight) pins

pumpkin-pricking tool, or large needle

lino (linoleum)-cutting tool

1. Trace a drawing of a cat (transcribe from one shown below) and enlarge. Fix the template over the base of the pumpkin with dressmaker's pins. Using the pumpkin-pricking tool or a large needle, make small pin pricks along all the lines.

2. Using the lino-cutting tool, and following the lines of the pin pricks, carve the design on to the pumpkin, starting with the main outlines. Cut shorter lines for the cat's fur.

TIP

The technique of decorating the surface of the pumpkin, rather than cutting it out, is easy to adapt to suit your preferred Halloween symbol.

Candle Holders

The firm flesh and rich colours of many autumn fruits and vegetables make them ideal for candle holders. Experiment with different shapes and colour.

4. Hollow out the centre of the gourd so that it is just large enough for the candle. Insert the candle.

5. For the squash candle holder, hollow out the centre of the squash using an apple corer and insert a green candle.

You will need

firm-fleshed fruit, such as apples,

gourds and squashes

night-lights (tea-lights) and

assorted candles

apple corer

sharp knife

raffia and autumn leaves

1. For the apple candle holder, slice a little off the bottom of the apple to get a stable base, then remove the core using a corer.

2. Using a corer or a sharp knife, make the hole just big enough to accommodate a night-light.

3. For the gourd candle holder, first wrap a large pillar candle in an autumn leaf, and secure with raffia. (Burn only large diameter candles wrapped in leaves as the outer surface is left cool.)

Autumn Apple Display

Crab apples have a special charm and the cultivated varieties produce fruit in a range of warm colours. They make wonderful material for wild-looking arrangements such as this candle ring.

You will need

25cm/10in diameter florist's foam ring

4 yellow ochre tapered candles

secateurs (pruners)

2 branches crab apples

3 branches pin oak (*Quercus palustris*) leaves

I. Soak the florist's foam ring. Set the candles, evenly spaced, into the foam. Using sharp secateurs, cut the small branches of crab apples off the main stems. Arrange the oak leaves around the ring, overlapping them to hide the foam.

2. When the ring is covered with oak leaves, add smaller sprays to the inside.

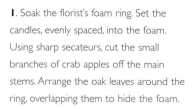

3. Add the bunches of crab apples.

TIP
Let the candle ring dry out for a lasting autumn arrangement.

Index